POSITIVE VIBES
~ 2 ~
"MAKING STRIDES"

PRESTON MITCHUM

ISBN: 978-1-941345-83-2

Canyon Lake, Texas
www.ErinGoBraghPublishing.com

INTRODUCTION

No matter what is going on around author Preston Mitchum, Jr., he is always looking for that positive perspective on the situation. He celebrates the good times and looks for ways to learn through the tough ones. In his second book, his message remains:

Positive Thoughts, Positive Vibes.

Having received such incredible feedback from his ever increasing number of readers and social media followers, Preston put pen to paper once again to bring you even more positivity in our ever-changing and sometimes tumultuous world.

Whether you read these messages back-to-back, or every once in a while, the goal is to help boost your perception of life, take time to appreciate it and find the positives that are all around us.

God has given us such an amazing gift - this life.

Let's show our appreciation for it by cherishing each and every moment.

TABLE OF CONTENTS

MAKING STRIDES

Today is the day you make the first step. God promised if you make the first step, He will make the second. You are making strides to add a little more positivity in your life. Join the positive vibes movement and continue to do the things you need to do to live the life you want.

Create that vibe tribe of genuine people and allow them to support and inspire you moving forward. Step one today, will lead to many more steps moving forward. Continue making strides and allow your passion for living your best life to shine.

POSITIVE THOUGHTS, POSITIVE VIBES!

NOTE TO SELF:

RELAX

IT'S ALL ABOUT BALANCE!

Your ability to grow comes from surrounding yourself with good people. Like-minded means people who think alike or have the same view point. We also need folks who think differently to challenge the norm.

It's all about balance! Opposites do attract but they find common ground in acceptance. Understanding one another is key to creating peaceful environments. Most people want the best for themselves and by releasing positive energy you will attract positive people.

Relax by the Fire

There is nothing like relaxing next to a nice fire. Grab some twigs, logs and start up the fire pit. You sit back and stare into the fire and you get away for a little while. Another opportunity has presented itself to breathe. Yes, summer nights can be muggy, but gaze onto the stars and allow your mind to relax. We all have different ways to relax, understanding what works for you is key. What gives you that moment to see and feel good? Life's problems, and the hustle and bustle of the world will be there when you get back.

DAY OF REST

Make today your day of rest. Some days you feel so tired, you can barely stand. The ability to get through your day and get into bed is the best feeling.

Your body and spirit need time to rest. Without rest, you find yourself spinning in circles without truly accomplishing the tasks at hand. Put a few things aside and take some time to breathe today.

Let your mind relax and fuel your spirit.

POSITIVE THOUGHTS, POSITIVE VIBES!

BE WITH NATURE

The great outdoors! My youngest son loves being outside. He finds joy in everything from catching bugs to looking for slugs late at night. Being outdoors makes him happy. God's little creatures can offer a sense of gratification. Go take a walk or sit on the porch.

Take a few minutes to enjoy the peacefulness of the outdoors. It's simplistic, no drama, no over thinking. Nature allows you to just be and enjoy what it has to offer. You might be surprised how good it makes your spirit feel.

DAILY AFFIRMATIONS

*When was the last time
you just listened?*

*Close your eyes for thirty
seconds and just listen. Cars.
Construction. Birds. Wind.
Every sound is a part of life.*

LET YOUR HEART BE AT HOME

They say home is where the heart is. My oldest son would ask, "Daddy, what are we doing today?" I would answer, "Not sure, what would you like to do?" He almost always says, "Stay home." There is a comfort in being in the space you call home - a place where you feel love, safe and at peace. Many of us search all of our lives looking for a place we can call home. Sometimes the space is right in front of you. The simplicity of it is what we should look for. Home is where the heart is and let your heart be at home.

Some Alone Time

There will be times when being alone is a good thing. Withdraw yourself from toxic people and situations. Allow your spirit some blessing time to rejuvenate your soul. We go through stages in life where we need to find ourselves again. Look within to see who the real you is and if you're ok with that. Alone time will let you revisit your inner self and focus on more positivity in your life.

POSITIVE THOUGHTS, POSITIVE VIBES!

TIME TO GET AWAY

It's time for you to get away. Nope, not a vacation to an exotic island with beautiful blue water. Get away from the negativity from within. The energy you have on the inside can be eating away at your very soul. It's not allowing you to breathe and swim your way through the waves. Negative thoughts, words and people are keeping you from your positive self.

That's right it's time to get away, so you can see the ocean from afar.

PEACE FROM WITHIN

Finding peace is not always easy. Sometimes, the ones around you can take away your peace. If that is the case, it may behoove you to lose communication with some of those around you. It may be easier said than done, but the benefit will be a great reward. Getting rid of the noise is the first step, which will allow the positive to come through. Too much negativity will not allow enough room for the positivity to move on it. Remember that peace begins from within. If your inside is not free of negativity, how can there be peace?

NEVER ENOUGH TIME

God gives us 24 hours, well maybe 12-16, to work. But it is still not enough to get everything done. Why do you have so many things to do? Why do we stress ourselves out with no relief, just to live?

Make a list of all the things you need to get done. Eliminate the ones that can wait until tomorrow and allow some time to relax? We must take time to be still and breathe. This provides the balance necessary to get all of those things done. Remember what you don't get done today will be there tomorrow and sometimes it's just not meant to get done.

DON'T STRESS

What are you stressing about? You have done all that you can and given your best. Not much more can be done. This means there is no need to keep stressing. We all have fifty million things to do with very little time. Maybe you need to minimize the things on your list or prioritize and put the most important things at the top.

I can tell you one thing: stress will not help. It blocks your mind and your ability to get things done.

WINNERS AND LOSERS

Does anyone really win or lose in life? What would you consider winning? Lots of money, fancy car, big house, lots of friends? Some people get lost in trying to win at life. They forget to live and appreciate what life has to offer through the process. Happiness comes in many forms but we know it starts from within.

A positive spirit can lead you to the happiness you seek. You could be winning right now and not even know it. Take a step back, breathe and feel the good all around you. You look like a winner to me.

PLAY!

Try this. Stand at a playground and watch the children play. The simplicity of it is beautiful. It doesn't matter the shade, height or even if they speak the same language - they play.

Play is an awesome way to communicate. It allows the spirit to be free. The goal is simple: have fun. When we look into the eyes of a child, the innocence in them is what life is all about.

Try not complicating what life has to offer. Focus on all of the positivity around you.

A CHILD'S LOVE

And a child shall lead them. One of the greatest gifts God gives us is children. Pure and innocent, they come into the world just needing love and guidance.

This is also one of the greatest responsibilities as well. As parents, you give your all and in return they give you unconditional love. Love for our children comes in all different forms and wanting the best for them is universal.

Allow their purity and innocence to help lead your steps. You will be surprised how much you will learn.

POSITIVE THOUGHTS, POSITIVE VIBES!

FINDING

YOUR

HAPPY

WHERE IS YOUR HAPPY PLACE?

You hear people talking about a happy place. What is that? An actual place you travel to for some peace and quiet? Could it be the beach, church, wooded area, etc. or is it something that you do? Being in a happy place or space is essential to creating balance in your life. Getting away from the hustle and bustle of the world allows you to feel peace. We all deserve that! It will allow us to give our best to the world. A happier you!

POSITIVE THOUGHTS, POSITIVE VIBES!

Finding Happiness

Where can you find happiness? We all want to be happy, right? What does happiness look or feel like? It includes positive thinking, pleasant emotions, and some form of satisfaction. Start with appreciation for the good in your life. Count your many blessings, some are as simple as waking up in the morning. Create that list of the things you want to accomplish. You are in charge of what your happiness looks and feels like. Just be and soak in all the good around you. Remember that your happiness comes from within.

FIND YOUR HAPPY PLACE

How cool is it that you have a happy place? Yes, we all need one. A place that provides peace in the midst of the storm. They call it 'Stormy Monday' as we all wait for Friday to come. That is not the way to live. We should love every day. Be able to enjoy the blessings of each day God gives us. Maybe you can transfer some of the awesome things about your happy place into day-to-day living. Peace can be found all around us if we just look for it. Push the negativity aside and allow happiness within yourself.

CHOOSE THE LIFE YOU LIVE

We all control the type of life we want to live. Most of us would love to live a happy life filled with positivity. Of course, there will be some bumps in the road, but our choices decide that. Also, things you have no control of will try to consume you. You decide what gets in the way of your happiness.

Take a few minutes every morning to balance yourself with positive thoughts that will keep you on the right path. Remember you have the power to live the life you want.

POSITIVE THOUGHTS, POSITIVE VIBES!

LAUGHTER IS YOUR MEDICINE

I had a great conversation yesterday with a good friend of mine and could not stop laughing. You know that slump over almost falling to the ground laughing. BeBe Winans said it best, "Laughter is Just a Medicine." We all need to have the kind of moments when the laughing never stops. Laughing will help you get those tough times. Those times when you are not feeling supported, if your heart is broken, or when it's a can't-find-your-smile kind of day. Take your medicine and get your laugh on, my friends. It's the perfect medicine that will make your mind, body and soul feel good.

DON'T LET ANYONE STEAL YOUR JOY

You hear it time and time again in church. Don't let anyone steal your joy. Well, how can you keep that from happening?

Do you even know what your joy is? What makes you feel good inside? First, figure that one out, then make sure to protect it. If it makes you smile, glow and energizes others, protect it. You will be tested by the ones who are not accepting of it. Your shine is not for everyone so protect it for the ones who deserve it. Don't let anyone steal your joy because someone out there is waiting for it.

*Consider it pure joy,
my brothers and sisters,
whenever you face trials of many kinds,
because you know that the testing of
your faith produces perseverance.
Let perseverance finish its work so that
you may be mature and complete,
not lacking anything.*

FEELING SAFE

When I look at my two sons, I marvel in their simplicity. Most of us adults don't get it, in the way they do. Our needs and wants are different. They want love, food, shelter, maybe a few pieces of candy and a toy or two. Feeling safe is most important. We should all take a moment to bask in the pure simplicity of living in the way they do. Life might not be as difficult if we keep it simple. Take what they give us from within and allow our growth to form from that.

WHAT KEEPS YOU
FROM YOUR HAPPY?

Why are so many people unhappy? What would make you happy? Love, money, less work and more vacation time? The stress of everyday living can weigh on the mind, body and soul. It can have you spinning in all different directions and keep you from your happiness.

They say, "Beauty is in the eye of the beholder." Well, happiness is too. You hold the key to your door of happiness. Look for the few simple things that make you happy and focus on them. You will be surprised how light your spirit will get and how peaceful you may feel.

Therefore I tell you, do not worry about your life, what you will eat or drink; or about your body, what you will wear. Is not life more than food, and the body more than clothes?

Look at the birds of the air; they do not sow or reap or store away in barns, and yet your heavenly Father feeds them. Are you not much more valuable than they?

Can any one of you by worrying add a single hour to your life?

I FOUND IT!

I found my path or at least the road I should travel. Man, I have lost a lot, cried a few tears and was unsure on a number of occasions. But today it feels good to know I'm where I need to be.

My mind, body and soul are in the right place and space. The feeling was uncomfortable, but I found my way through it. God has a pathway, road, or journey just for you. Believe it and keep moving forward because the only person stopping you, is you.

POSITIVE THOUGHTS, POSITIVE VIBES!

CLEANING

HOUSE

WHO ARE YOU, REALLY?

Do people change? Do they offer their true selves or is it a façade? Yes, people change, and sometimes we never really know who they are. Everyone is different and some people never show their true colors. They say some of us are an open book. We allow you to fully understand who and what we are. Change is in the eye of the beholder. If change is true, then let it be, but if not, then the truth will come through. If not, then maybe you never really got their true spirit. Either way you will find out.

POSITIVE THOUGHTS, POSITIVE VIBES!

CREATE CHANGE

Circumstances can change your life in the blink of an eye. Don't let adversity steer your spirit into a different direction. This storm shall pass and another one will come. It's up to you to see the big picture and figure out how to handle the situation when it arises. You can create change by looking at your circumstances from a different perspective. See the good first and let that be your driving force. Surround yourself with people who inspire your spirit and offer help in your time of need. From within you have the power to shine no matter what you are going through.

POSITIVE THOUGHTS, POSITIVE VIBES!

CHANGE YOUR PERSPECTIVE

If you think most things are terrible or just not your cup of tea you may need to look within. Terrible is all in the mind. It's all how you view it or take it in.

Stop looking for the negative and find a little good. Nothing is perfect and some things will just be downright awful. Today, you have the power to change your perspective and perception. It's all in your mind and it's time to allow your heart to step in. Use a combination of mind, body and soul and see the positivity shine through.

POSITIVE THOUGHTS, POSITIVE VIBES!

MAKE ROOM FOR GOOD

I was driving down the street and Jonathan McReynolds said, "I will make room for you." Today is the day when you can move it over. You have to allow space for the good to come in. Negativity will take over and not allow your mind, body and soul to be still. In order to see and feel your blessing you need some still time. Push aside as much as you can and let the good that is there for you shine through. Make the first step and God will help with the next one.

POSITIVE THOUGHTS, POSITIVE VIBES!

CHANGE COMES IN ALL FORMS

Just because it works for you doesn't mean it will work for someone else. We all have our own road and journey to travel. It's hard enough to make our own life changes so trying to help or guide others can be difficult.

Our changes come at the right time and we have to be in the right space to accept them. Someone else might not be there yet. So, when offering advice and suggestions to others, take that into consideration. Change comes in all forms and someone else's change might not be yours to handle.

YOUR HOME

They say home is where the heart is. My oldest son, Carter, will ask "Daddy, what are we doing today?" I answer, "Not sure, what would you like to do?" He replies, "Stay home."

There is a comfort in being in the space you call home. It is a place where you feel love, safe and at peace.

Many of us search all of our lives looking for a place we can call home. Sometimes, the space in right in front of you. The simplicity of it is what we should look for.

Home is where the heart is so let your heart be at home.

POSITIVE THOUGHTS, POSITIVE VIBES!

UNDERSTANDING RELATIONSHIPS

I get it. Sometimes you can love someone deeply, and not really like them. In a world filled with many different personalities we are bound to need space from people.

Once you're able to breathe, you could find yourself feeling different about the person. Taking the time to understand the relationship you have with that person is key. You might not need to like the ones you love or love the ones you like all of the time. Letting it just be, could be the best thing.

POSITIVE THOUGHTS, POSITIVE VIBES!

THINK FOR YOURSELF!

Stop allowing others to control your thoughts. Think for yourself! Be you and love who you are today and who you are becoming. Surround yourself with people who believe in and love you, for you. If it's not the case for you, then you're not around the right people.

We should be lifting each other up and enhancing each other's lives. People should make you feel good about who you are. Offer constructive criticism without judgment. You can control your surroundings, which means you can control who is in your orbit!

POSITIVE THOUGHTS, POSITIVE VIBES!

ASK FOR HELP

The ability to accept help is not always easy. It is not easy to open up and allow people in. We all have our reasons for it. We tell ourselves, "I can do it all by myself." We don't always know how to ask for help, or have a hard time verbalizing our needs. They say sometimes asking for help can be the bravest thing you can do.

Surround yourself with good people who you can feel comfortable with in your time of need. We all need someone at some point to assist us and yes, it ok to say, "I need help." By asking for help you start the process of taking care of you. And yes, we all need the best you have to offer.

Break Through the Noise

I've got joy deep down in my soul. What could give you joy that feels that good? In most cases, it is something simple! A sunset, a walk by the lake, a smile or hug from that special someone.

It's usually the little things in life that bring us joy. Today you might be having a hard time finding or feeling that joy. It's there, you just got caught up in the noise. Break through the noise. Turn down the volume, get through the noise and get back to the joy. Take a moment to feel from within.

Never allow the noise to steal your joy!

*May the God of hope fill you
with all joy and peace
as you trust in him,
so that you may overflow
with hope by the power
of the Holy Spirit.*

GET READY TO SWING

You have questions but no one seems to have the answers. It's just life! Sometimes life can be full of questions with very few answers. You muddled through some days just trying to figure things out. Why me? When will it end? Where should I go and to whom can I turn?

God might have the answers or at least a place of rest while you figure things out. Life will throw you a few curve balls, but God can help you hit one right out of the park. It might just have to be on His time and terms. Be patient and wait for the right pitch before you swing. That ball is coming.

GOD WITH ANOTHER O IS GOOD

In order for a fresh start, the mind, body and soul needs cleansing. The song sung by Shirley Caesar said it best, "Lord if you find anything that is not like you, take it away."

Ask God to participate in your clearing promise. My oldest son, Carter, says often, God with another "o" is good. So if God is good why not add him to the process. A fresh start is not an easy task but having as much good as possible in the mix will help. Move forward, mix in good people, and let God order your steps. If it's not good, ask him to take it away!

ACCEPTING

THE PAST

THE PAST DOESN'T DEFINE YOU

I have made some mistakes in my life. I didn't always have what we would call the right answer. Would I change the past? Nope! You know why? Because the past doesn't define me, but it has shaped my present.

I have learned from my mistakes and continue down my road called "growth." We grow and through growth we become the people we are today. So yes, I made some mistakes, but I now have the ability to look at them from a different perspective. This new me will be better than ever.

KEEP YOUR PROMISES

In our life time we will come across false promises. People will make promises that they cannot or choose not to keep. How important is it to keep your promise? Is your word your bond? Sometimes we make the mistakes of making promises when we just need to keep it real. Don't stress about making everyone happy. Superheroes are not needed all the time. The only promise you need to keep is giving your best.

POSITIVE THOUGHTS, POSITIVE VIBES!

WHAT'S IN YOUR BACKPACK?

All of us are carrying stuff around. Stuff from our past. Now is the time to clean out that backpack so it doesn't go with you into the future.

Things from the past have shaped you but do not define you. You can learn, embrace and let go of the things weighing you down.

Lighten the load so that your spirit can be free. Freeing your spirit will allow your light to shine and hopefully put the past behind you so you can start living in the here and now.

FORGIVE AND NOT FORGET?

How do we free ourselves from hate and anger? Both can eat away at your soul and not allow you to move forward. They say you must forgive, but sometimes you just don't know how. Forgive and not forget?

Today is the day you take control of how you view the situation. You can forgive, so you can move forward. It's in the past for a reason and now you live in the present. Smile at the hate and laugh at the anger. Your positivity will overcome negativity any day.

FEELING, ALLOWS US TO GROW

Look into the eyes and see the soul. You wear your heart on your sleeve. Are you allowing people to feel and experience the true you? They say sometimes you can stand next to a person and feel their spirit. Is it good or bad? Broken or healed?

It's ok to let people in, because you can control how they make you feel. Connection comes through feeling, and feeling allows us to grow. Those experiences of sharing who we are, allow us to be at peace. Accepting what we give to the world is pretty darn good. Bring on the good, and heal the broken.

DON'T BE
AFRAID TO LIVE

Deep down inside is a fear, a fear to live. Fear of the unknown, the things you might hold deep within. The experiences you go through can create an unsafe place inside your mind. You grasp for things, people and places that will help provide that safe place. Past experiences might be holding you back from becoming the you that you want to be. Trust and have faith that God has a plan for you. He will not let you face more than you can handle. Today is the day to face your fears.

DON'T TAKE IT PERSONALLY

Come on, stop taking things personally. We all have to put our egos aside. Someone's projection could be a reflection on them. You can deflect the negative and find the positive in how you allow it to affect you. You have control on how things make you feel. Take a step back and understand before you react. If someone is trying to be cruel or harmful, deflect. You know you. Let that be what you feel. Let your light shine and glare out the darkness.

POSITIVE THOUGHTS, POSITIVE VIBES!

FACE YOUR FEAR

Do you stare fear in the face? You have to look deep within and use your past experience for strength.

It's not easy to do or attempt something you fear. Taking the leap is not easy but the outcome could be worth it.

You will never know what you can do unless you try. Through this process you will find out more about yourself. Build confidence in the old and new you.

POSITIVE THOUGHTS, POSITIVE VIBES.

YOUR LOVE AND UNITY!

In this crazy world we live in, sometimes we forget that love conquers hate and unity eliminates division. We must be open to building bridges, instead of perpetuating hate, anger and ignorance.

Through love comes understanding and the ability to see past ourselves. We cannot let our egos cloud a pathway of being open-minded.

You control what you feel for others. Can you see their beauty or just their faults? Can you see beyond what might hurt and see what can heal?

Start with positivity and see what you get!

POSITIVE THOUGHTS, POSITIVE VIBES!

FiGHT ON

A song in my rotation includes the phrase, "you fight on." Trouble doesn't always last, but I hear you. You have been knocked down, felt alone, stumbled a few times but yes, "you fight on." You fight on because today and every day you continue to work towards being and giving your best. Sing that song that lifts your spirit, wear that smile and let your light shine. You have been through tough times before, so today and every day, allow the positive in and it will help you fight on.

POSITIVE THOUGHTS, POSITIVE VIBES!

TIRED OF BEING TIRED?

Fannie Mae Hamer said it best. She was tired of fighting a fight that seemed to be unwinnable. But she kept fighting.

You do the same thing day in and day out. What are you fighting for? A better life, family or just the ability to find peace? When we see the big picture, the fight is worth it. You will be tired and have times when you want to give up. But today is not that day because the big picture tells you to press on. There is a light at the end of the tunnel.

TRUST

The word, "trust" may not be a friend of yours. What does it mean to trust or be trusted? We give of ourselves and have no choice but to trust. We have to trust in others, ourselves and the universe that some good will come from it.

But what happens when it doesn't? When the word trust is not too friendly? How do you trust again, repair and move forward? You do because moving forward is all you can do. Not everything or everyone is untrusting. The ups and downs are a part of life. Push the non-trusting aside today and keep it moving.

IT'S COMPLICATED!

You were once in love and now, you are out of love. Your mind, body and soul are in a different place. It's complicated.

The reason it's complicated, you want to share yourself. You want someone to know, like, love and accept the true you. The question is, are you loving yourself first? Some call it self-care, loving yourself so that your true light will shine. As you continue to love yourself, you will become the best you. Sharing yourself with the right person or persons will get easier.

WOE IS ME

Here you go again, feeling sorry for yourself. The "woe is me," song is playing loud in the background. Don't wait around for anyone to listen because everyone is feeling it too. You got this! Troubles don't last, this too shall pass.

Take a step back and reapproach the situation. Try to see it differently in hopes of finding some positivity or the silver lining. It's there but sometimes we don't see it because we're not really looking. We're stuck in the, "woe is me." It's time to get up and see your way through this one. You will be surprised at yourself.

POSITIVE THOUGHTS, POSITIVE VIBES!

FOCUS

ON

YOU

DETOUR NOW

You did it! You took a step back and with that, now you get it. The real meaning in life is not what you have but what you don't have. What you can't see because the road ahead is closed. You need a detour to take you down a path of open mindedness. Being closed minded will keep you from receiving the blessing right in front of you. You have the power to change how you think and see the world. Pause every once and awhile to see what you might be missing.

LOVE YOURSELF

It all starts with loving yourself. How the heck do we do that? I mean, in the crazy world we live in, loving yourself can get lost. Love the uniqueness of you and allow that light to shine. God made you in the image he wanted so, embrace it my friend. Think about all of the wonderful things you already offer to the world. Give from your heart, feel from your soul and speak without ill intent. Your ability to love is already there you just need to start from within and appreciate all the awesomeness you have to offer. You are beautiful on the inside and out. Believe it, own it and share it!

WHAT INSPIRES YOU?

Who or what inspires You? We talk about it often. Who you decide to surround yourself with is key. Who you allow in your space can provide the spark or inspiration you need.

Pause for a second and take in the many things around you that keep you going. Things like reading, medication, exercise and nutrition can really feed your soul. Take care of your mind, body and soul first which will allow for the awakening. You will then be able to really see and feel who or what inspires you.

IT'S ALL ABOUT YOU

You know what? Today it's all about You!

Today is the day you will look deep down within and focus on you. Not your friend's problems or issues but the things you want to tweak about yourself.

We all have those little things we want to work on about ourselves. Today is the day. It's ok to tell your friends that it's self-care day and it will just have to wait. Allowing your light to shine brighter is like wearing glory for the world to see.

POSITIVE THOUGHTS, POSITIVE VIBES!

HEAL YOURSELF

How do we heal ourselves? At some point in our lives the road will get pretty rocky. The other side of the storm is a place of healing.

The healing process has already started working, you just need to recognize it and own it. The tough times we go through, will form and shape us in ways that sometimes we have no control over. Look for blessings, find the positive and allow healing to occur. You might just find out some cool things about yourself you had no idea were there.

YOUR PURPOSE

What is your purpose in life? It's a question that seems difficult to answer sometimes. Our purpose in life lies within our passion. What are you passionate about?

Today is the day you jot down a few notes and tap into your passion. It may be gardening, design, cooking, exercise, or something else. Find your purpose in life by following your passion. Share your gifts with the world and allow your light to shine.

THE RIGHT OUTLOOK

Change your attitude and change your life. Debbie Downer should not be hanging around for long. Life is waiting for you to live it but what if your attitude stinks. Why are you unhappy? What things need to change to get you on the right path? Well, your chance of getting there starts with your attitude.

Allow your attitude to take you places that you have never been before. Allow it to attract the people you want in your life. Anything is possible with the right outlook on life. It's time to make the change!

PAUSE THE PRIORITIES

We know all about priorities right? Priorities can drive us crazy trying to get everything accomplished. Some days it feels like you're losing your marbles. Remember not to let those urgent things crowd the important ones. Take a moment to breathe and understand what you can and cannot do. Some people travel the world looking for what they need and miss out on what they already have at home. Time will pass you by trying to get everything done so pause and make sure your priorities don't get in the way of living and loving life.

WRITE IT DOWN

We all have goals in life. What are yours? Do you know? If not, get out that pen and paper and start writing. Finish school, career change, fall in love, whatever it might be, write it down.

It all starts with making a list and getting things started. Then you will need to put yourself around people who can ignite that fire. It's called inspiration! Putting yourself around inspiring people will help get you going in the right direction. Your goals are possible with the right plan and support. Get yourself a good mix!

INVITE THE RIGHT LOVE IN

Song by The Moments say, "I found love on a two way street and lost it on a lonely highway". Love can be found on many different roads or maybe one road with a few pot holes. Have you looked within? Did you truly have Love? Were you complete enough to find the one that would complement you?

Sometimes we need to be in the right place and space to invite the right love in. True love will enhance what you have already presented and allow that to continue its growth. Be patient and fine tune you first.

FILL YOUR CUP

You hear it over and over again, "misery loves company." Well, I'm sorry, I don't want that company. Try avoiding the negative energy. Try avoiding those people and situations if possible. If you can't find a positive outlook then move on to something else.

Negativity can become contagious and the last thing you need is to catch something else. Your life is already fully packed with stuff to do and take care of. Go search for some positive juice today and drink until your cup runs full.

POSITIVE THOUGHTS, POSITIVE VIBES!

NEVER GIVE UP

I'm telling you to never give up on you. Don't throw in the towel. It's tough, you turn to the left and right and nothing is working out. Your friends are few and far between. It's ok, because this is life. You are being tested and it's time to look within, my friend. Like the song says, "trouble don't last always," and today is your day. You are still standing because something about you doesn't quit. Look for and think of something positive and start with that. Your view point and perspective can provide what you need to keep moving forward.

POSITIVE THOUGHTS, POSITIVE VIBES!

The Real You

It's time to put who you were, behind you and find out who you are. Most of us spend our lives not truly knowing who we are. You take care of this and that, please others and become Mr. or Ms. Dependable. The you gets lost in the sauce.

It's time to stir things up and look within to see the true you. Your light is ready to shine if you can open the blinds. The world needs to have the real you so that the ones who need your blessing will receive it. We all have something to offer and let's make it as pure and true as possible.

GRACE

Because of grace, I stand here today! What is grace? Grace gets me through my struggles. Grace allows me to be me. You accepted this imperfect person and say it's ok. It's ok to be you, because God has got your back.

Grace allows us to give the world the best we have to offer and fine tune those things we need to. God loves us for who we are and he wants you to stand tall and love who you are today. Today is your day to love you!

POSITIVE THOUGHTS, POSITIVE VIBES!

WHOSE PLAN IS IT?

You have a plan and God has a plan. Which one is best? You woke up this morning moving forward with your plan. Things rolling right along until that bump in the road that throws things off the path. You're not sure which way to turn and what the next move should be. That's when you ask God for help. You ask for help with your current plan but He has another.

Having faith will allow you to detour into God's plan for you. It allows Him to order your steps and lead the way. It will smooth things out in time. Be still and let the winds from up above put your spirit on the right path.

Therefore,
my dear brothers and sisters,
stand firm.
Let nothing move you.
Always give yourselves fully
to the work of the Lord,
because you know that your labor
in the Lord is not in vain.

Finding

Real

Connections

STRIKE UP A CONVERSATION

Sometimes it's worth talking to a stranger. You don't know the person in line at the store, the person on the bus, or at the football game. But the person next to you can offer a refreshing spirit that can brighten up your day. It's simple. No judgement, no objective, no need. Just connection. An opportunity to strike up a conversation about anything can lead to a moment. That's a moment for you to be you and share the positivity you have to offer. Enjoy the moment and let time be still within the conversation of a stranger.

WHEN STRANGERS BECOME FRIENDS

You call that person your friend who was once a stranger. You connected for a reason. How we view, interrupt or accept the connection is up to us. We need to allow ourselves to be vulnerable and open to the unlimited possibilities of the connection.

We were all strangers at one point and allowed ourselves to feel, like, love and acquire a friendship with someone. Being open to the connection can take your mind, body and soul to new heights.

LIKE-MINDED PEOPLE

You want to be loved and accepted but no one gets you. What? Are you that difficult to understand? You don't look like you're from outer space. The issue could be the people you're around. They say surround yourself with like-minded people. Folks that you have the same views and likes that you have.

Maybe by making a few adjustments, you might come across a few folks that 'get you'. If you're willing to open up it will get easier. The chances are more on the positive side of people seeing the real you.

A REAL CONNECTION

A simple encounter can lead to friendship for life. You had no idea that the person you just met would have your back for life. Why do we connect with some and not others? What makes a connection special or above the rest?

We see similarities in people that draw us in. It could be a spiritual, work, or other connection. There are many different reasons why we connect. The spirit of that person could be easy like Sunday morning. If the connection is real, then just looking within will provide the answer. We met for a reason and our connection has purpose. Enjoy the simplicity of it.

A friend loves at all times,
and a brother is born
for a time of adversity.

THE POWER OF INTIMACY

The connection between two people can add positivity to one's life. One can define intimacy as, any action that enhances the mind/heart connection between two people. Even just sitting quietly holding hands is intimate with the right person.

Connection is important. It allows the mind, body and soul to grow and evolve. Be willing to feel the intimacy one has to offer and enjoy the beauty it holds.

SHOW YOUR LOVE

Saying, "I love you," can come in many different forms. Sometimes we don't say it or show it enough. We all get caught up in the rat race of life. There is always too much to do with too little time. Appreciating the people in your circle can sometimes take a back seat.

Find a way to show your love so even when you don't say it people feel it. Live a life filled with it so, "I Love You," will shine brightly from your spirit. When a person can feel it, that can mean more than saying it.

POSITIVE THOUGHTS, POSITIVE VIBES!

DAILY AFFIRMATIONS

Show Gratitude!

*Take the time today to tell
or show someone
you appreciate them.*

Tomorrow is not promised!

REASSURANCE

There will be times in our lives when the word *reassurance* will appear. Our vulnerability will provide an opportunity for someone or something to make you feel safe, less afraid, upset or have doubt.

When someone provides that reassurance, that who you are and what you have to offer is just right, your comfort level will grow and your doubt will fade. This reassurance will give you the chance to be the true you. That's right the true you is what the world needs.

YOUR RELATIONSHIP WITH GOD

One of the greatest gifts my mother gave me was an introduction to God. There is importance in having a relationship with the creator of the universe. That relationship has taken on many forms over the years.

When I discuss having a relationship with God amongst others I relay that it's your own personal relationship. It belongs to you. It's not what others want it to be. It is yours and yours alone. Whether it's a happy time or a time of need, God comes to you in the way He chooses. Hold strong to this and let the light God has for you shine through.

Be on your guard;
stand firm in the faith;
be courageous;
be strong.
Do everything in love.

ASK GOD FOR HELP

Just when one thing goes right another goes wrong. You just can't get ahead and the light at the end of the tunnel is dim. How can you breathe when it never stops?

Did you ask God for help? You can talk to Him and He will hear you. He might send you an angel. Allow your mind to rest for a bit and give you the strength to get through it. Asking God for help allows your mind to pause and focus on Him. This might be the little thing you need to reevaluate and increase your faith.

WHO IS IN YOUR CORNER?

We will meet many people in our lifetime but who is truly there for you? How will you know? When times are tough or going well who can you turn too when all heck breaks loose? Can they lift your spirits and help you through it?

We all will need someone to be there when we need them most. An angel will be waiting in the wings. The key is to be open minded when they show up. It could be the one you least expect and the beauty in that is priceless. So who is truly in your corner?

COMMUNICATION

You may ask yourself how you can communicate better and have a truly good conversation? Well communicating is easy, right? You just talk, say what's on your mind and people will understand. Not so fast there, it takes more than that. We must be able to listen, feel and articulate what's on our mind.

Trying to interpret what someone is trying to say isn't always easy. We all have different ways of communicating and the willingness to understand each other is key. Taking the time to listen and talking through it can provide a positive outcome in the situation.

ENERGY

IS

CONTAGIOUS

ENERGIZE YOURSELF

You get up every morning and you give it your all. Consider giving it 100% or close to it. Yet, you discover that is not enough or people still need more. Are you putting your energy in the wrong people or places? Do you feel drained or inspired to give more? Take a step back and analyze the steps you are taking. Make sure balance is a part of your daily vocabulary. Without balance you will feel drained. Don't allow too much taking without giving. Take some time out to energize yourself. Give but be cautious in where and to whom you might be giving to.

POSITIVE THOUGHTS, POSITIVE VIBES!

ENERGIZE YOUR MIND

Attraction starts from within. Physical attraction is common but mental attraction can be hard to find. That person that makes your heart sing and your spirit soar. How does your spirit feel when you speak or are in the presence of that person?

Do they energize your mind, body and soul in ways that the physical cannot? Yes, we all enjoy a physical attraction but without the mental, the physical will fade. Surround yourself with people that simulate your mind which in turn will fuel your spirit.

POSITIVE THOUGHTS, POSITIVE VIBES!

GET YOUR BOOGIE DOWN

I think Al Jarreau said it best, "You can be what you want to. All you need is to get your boogie down." Sounds like you might need a few new moves or a change of pace. Getting stuck in your comfort or safe zone might not be what's best. I get it -- change is scary, darn right frightening sometimes, but you want peace, happiness and to feel free.

Put a plan together, start with small steps which might lead to a pretty good groove. We can't wait to see what your 'boogie down' looks like. The world is waiting for the best you that you have to offer and getting out of your comfort zone might be the answer.

Refuel Yourself

They say always give 100%, well today maybe 75% is all you have. Let that be enough for today and use the other 25% as fuel for tomorrow. "There's never enough time." Well, enough time for what? Sometimes good enough is good enough.

Don't continue to push yourself to the limit with no room to breathe. Remember giving your all is not always easy. You give your best day in and day out and today you did the same. Recharge up and refuel!

POSITIVE THOUGHTS, POSITIVE VIBES!

DAILY AFFIRMATIONS

*This world wants you to stay
busy all the time. There is no time
to just sit and be still.
Take a few minutes
to tap in today!*

POSITIVE ENERGY

Who do you look up to? A role model, person you admire or one who inspires you? We are surrounded by all types of people. You can choose whom you would like to be in your circle or orbit.

Make sure the one you look up to is feeding you the positivity that you need. Feed off of the ones who inspire you and allow that to fuel your fire from within. Our spirit needs to feed off of good energy and yes that can come from many sources including the ones you look up too.

FREE YOURSELF

Mary Mary said it best, "take the shackles off my feet so I can dance." Free yourself from the negative energy of the world. The people in your circle could be holding you back from your blessing. Those feet of yours would love to shuffle or even do the twist but Chubby Checker can't help you with this one.

Take the next step, identify the people and things that are holding you back. Make the change towards positive living. It will not be easy but it will be necessary in order for you to step out onto the dance floor ahead.

ARE YOU READY?

There are such a thing as angels. In your time of need someone or something will appear. Not sure what form or shape but yes, an angel. A form of love will appear that will comfort the soul and rejuvenate the spirit. Are you ready?

Sometimes we're not ready to take in what the angel has to offer. The vulnerability of a person might just allow them to see and feel the security that angel offers. We all need a helping hand, someone or something that will be there for us at the right time.

The beauty is in recognizing it and appreciating it.

THE POWER OF A HUG!

There's nothing like a good hug from someone with positive energy. It can go through you and make everything ok. I know some of you don't like to be touched. Touch shows that someone cares, so you need to open up and allow that in.

A hug from the right person can make a world of difference. It's an unspoken gesture that offers comfort and makes the soul feel good. You must remember it's very important to take care of your soul. If your inside feels good then your outside will shine. And yes, we all need to see that light of yours shining bright.

POSITIVE THOUGHTS, POSITIVE VIBES!

*D*AILY *A*FFIRMATIONS

Share some love and
Be a light today!

Let your light shine!

UNDERSTAND YOURSELF

We spend so much time trying to change people or hoping they will be more like us. You cannot change the people around you, but you can change the people you choose to be in your circle. Understanding ourselves better will allow our spirit to attract the right people to be in our space. If someone wants to change it will be up to them to do so.

Focus on fine tuning you, which will open the doors for the right people to walk in. It's all about the energy you give out and watch what comes back in.

POSITIVE THOUGHTS, POSITIVE VIBES!

SMILE WITH YOUR EYES

I might be wearing a mask but I can smile with my eyes. I might not be able to give a hug but I can offer a kind word. During these tough times we have found creative ways to be kind. Sending gifts, posting positive messages on social media, video chats and doing drive by birthday parties are nice. The ability to give back and letting your kindness shine doesn't have to stop. We will always be able to adapt to change and we have done it together.

Through the struggles, we learn more about ourselves which will fuel the positive energy leading us in the future.

I HEAR YA!

You had your life all planned out and it's not looking anything like you imagined. Married, kids, successful job, big house, fancy car, etc. The issue is you were moving too fast.

Remember that living in the now is always the best because we cannot predict the future. When we move too fast we forget to see all of the awesome things around us now.

You have the power to control the present which might help with the future. Live, love and enjoy what you have now and allow that positive energy to lead you into the future.

POSITIVE THOUGHTS, POSITIVE VIBES.

YOUR ACTIONS SPEAK

Practice what you preach. Talk is cheap. Actions speak louder than words. The list goes on but you know what I'm trying to say. Be You! We spend so much time trying to please everyone else. Hoping everyone is happy with what we're offering. Just make sure you offer the true you. If you believe in you then your actions will speak loudly and clearly. Be the person that you want the world to know. Don't be afraid if someone will like it or not. Not everyone will feel your spirit. Let your actions speak louder than their words!

POSITIVE THOUGHTS, POSITIVE VIBES!

REJOICE ALWAYS

Rejoice always, pray continually,
give thanks in all circumstances;
for this is God's will for you
in Christ Jesus.

THE

NEW

YOU

BLESS THE WORLD WITH YOU

You woke up this morning and finally realized you have been giving the world second best. What happen to the best you have to offer or the best of you? Are you lost in the sauce, swimming around wondering where you went? The good part is you can start today finding you, the true and real you.

Start pleasing you first and the awesome light you have will shine bright. It's time to start blessing the world with the best you.

POSITIVE THOUGHTS, POSITIVE VIBES!

YOUR WAY OR...

You gotta do it your way! Today you're not listening to anyone else's suggestions or ideas. You've got all the answers and when things go wrong it's someone else's fault. Well it looks like you need a new outlook. Don't wait until the "stuff" hits the fan before you understand it's time to open up.

Allow others to assist, offer opinions and add a little something. Get that pot mixing with tons of variety. Your way or the highway might not work this time. Let's open up and add a little something different. You might be pleasantly surprised.

DETOUR NOW

You did it! You took a step back and with that now you get it. The real meaning in life is not what you have but what you don't have. What you can't see because the road ahead is closed.

You need a detour to take you down a path of open mindedness. Being closed minded will keep you from receiving the blessing right in front of you. You have the power to change how you think and see the world.

Pause every once and awhile to see what you might be missing.

THE ROAD TRAVELED

It's not about the destination, but the road traveled. It's not about where you are going but how you get there. That includes all of the pit stops and fill-ups along the way. These things help shape and prepare you for what is waiting.

Things always have a way of working themselves out. The pot holes, road closures and detours are a part of the journey. Continue to move forward and stay focused. You will be surprised where the road leads you.

POSITIVE THOUGHTS, POSITIVE VIBES.

AN HONEST APOLOGY

We use the words, "I'm sorry" often enough. Apologies can sometimes be short lived if the actions don't follow. They say if a person doesn't change their behavior then why apologize?

Are we using the word sorry to make ourselves feel ok about our actions? Or are we really honest about changing our behavior to match the words we say and use. I guess time will tell if the words match the action. They say your word is your bond, so hold true to you.

YOUR NEW DANCE

Yes, my friends, I'm not tired yet. They sang that song in church growing up -- hand clapping, foot stomping, singing and smiling. Nothing but joy and positive energy flowing throughout the building. I hear ya -- you have been knocked around, can't find your way, or not sure who to call when you need a friend. You're not tired yet because you have been through the struggle before. I can see you still standing trying to get stronger day by day.

Today you look within for the strength to get through this as well. Come on, get up, start that hand clapping, foot stomping, do a dance and sing that song! I can see your glow shining through. You're not tired yet because God just gave you a new dance.

Be strong and take heart,
all you who hope in the LORD.

Pop Up – Dive In

In the movie Lion Guard Bunga sang "Zuka Zama". It's a funny little song with lots of meaning. In Swahili it means, "Pop up, dive in."

Today may be your day to pop up and dive in. Dive in and let your heart sing and your soul feel. Open up and breathe new air and new life in the old life you have been living. Love the new life that's in right in front of you. Sing that song, dance that dance. Zuka Zuma might just be the song you need to wake up and dive in.

POSITIVE THOUGHTS, POSITIVE VIBES!

YOUR INNER CIRCLE

They thought they had you down for the count. You know the ones that call you to see if you're doing not so well. We have folks around us that look for the bad and forget about the good.

Well, it's time, my friends, to change that inner circle. Surround yourself with people who lift your spirit, rejuvenate your soul and stimulate your mind. It's a new day with a new outlook on life. It's all because you made changes to your environment in a positive way.

APPRECIATION

Today I will make sure to appreciate everything that I have and I am. Yesterday was a crazy day filled with drama, uncertainty, stress but also some joys. Let's focus on those joys and allow that to start our day.

Today you will make sure to take a few minutes to be thankful for what you have and who you are. Start with some positivity and allow that to help you with the other stuff.

POSITIVE THOUGHTS, POSITIVE VIBES!

Give thanks to the LORD, for he is good; his love endures forever.

DAILY AFFIRMATIONS

Be Thankful

What are you thankful for?
Take some time today and reflect
on the things that are
most important!

HELPING

OTHERS

HELP. DON'T ENABLE

There is a huge difference between helping others and enabling others. We have to take a step back to see if the help we are offering is beneficial. Someone might just need to feel a little fire to get going.

Holding folks accountable for their actions is not always a bad thing. Make sure the help you are offering will allow that person to be their own person. Don't allow a draining process to take place where they feed off your spirit. Life is all about balance. We need to keep ourselves well balanced in order to see the difference.

POSITIVE THOUGHTS, POSITIVE VIBES!

SOMEONE NEEDS YOU

Scared to let people get to know you? Some people might be shy, bashful or introverted. Maybe the issue is every time you give you get hurt. People don't know how to appreciate who you are. So they try to change you, put you down and put a dimmer on your light.

Well dimming the light won't work today because God made you in his image. Greatness is all over you and you must continue to share yourself. Someone out there needs your spirit. They need to see your smile. Because today your smile looks brighter than ever.

POSITIVE THOUGHTS, POSITIVE VIBES!

BE KIND

Today is your day to be kind. A single act of kindness can have a positive rippling effect.

Share of yourself and the next person may share with someone else. People talk about karma. What we do now can come back to affect us later.

It's not about being self-absorbed but rather, giving of yourself which will allow a peaceful spirit to take over. Being kind frees your spirit and unlocks the chains and negativity.

POSITIVE THOUGHTS, POSITIVE VIBES.

LET YOUR LIGHT SHINE

Wake up and decide to be you. That's right, I'm going to offer the world the real deal. I'm not going to sit and wonder if people will like it or not.

Is what I have to offer worthy enough? I need to make everyone happy with what they see on the outside. Your mindset may be in the wrong place. It's on the outside and you already forgot about the inside. That's where the real you is! Let that light shine baby and attract the ones who deserve it. If it works for them that's cool. If not, keep on keeping on!

OFFER THE BEST YOU

Are you wondering why the things you used to do are not happening anymore? How is your spirit? Are you broken? The world has worn you out and you can't find your juice.

Is it possible to break away from the rat race for a little? Can you clear your thoughts to get back to you? In order to offer the best you, you must get back to you. The things that gave you peace need to find a place in your heart again. Piece by piece today is your day to do and be you.

POSITIVE THOUGHTS, POSITIVE VIBES!

WHAT HAVE YOU GOT TO OFFER?

They say your beauty is in your openness. Yes you are real and offer yourself in a way to be appreciated and accepted. You can be straight forward and kind at the same time.

The beauty of all of this, is giving the world a chance to feel the real you. Openness can be a very powerful thing, allowing others in to accept what you have to offer. Through this you allow, attract and distract the ones who enter your orbit. Embrace the power and enjoy the beauty of being you. It has a place within the right space.

RAISE SOMEONE UP

Raise someone up, please! We spend so much time focusing on our own needs that we need to help someone else, too. It doesn't take much; a listening ear, a kind word or just spending a little time. Reach out and offer a helping hand to a friend in need. Ask someone how they are truly feeling and listen without judgment or opinion. It feels great making someone else feel good and it will give your spirit a positive boost!

POSITIVE THOUGHTS, POSITIVE VIBES!

WHEN

CHANGE

HAPPENS

WHAT IS YOUR TESTIMONY?

We have all been through the fire and prayed for rain. What is your testimony? Where have you come from to take you to the place you must go? Do you even know where you would like to be? What does the present look like to lead you into the future?

They say trouble doesn't last and we all have a story to share. Share your testimony so that it might help someone else get through their storm. Wash away some of those troubles with a little inspiration.

PEACE IS NEEDED

The loss of a loved one changes us. In some ways we can't always explain. Hurt, pain, sorrow and anger can consume us during that time. To ease the emotions people tell us to think about the good times.

How do we deal with it all? How do we allow our soul to grieve in peace? Remember that the spirit lives on. Why not have a chat with that loved one. I talk to my daddy every day. I ask him to guide my steps. Some might say that's silly for a 46 year old, but it gives me peace.

Peace in the midst of the journey is just what might be needed.

YOUR ENLIGHTENMENT

We talk about being enlightened or the enlightenment. Your spiritual growth allows for a deeper awareness of you who are. We would all love to know our purpose in life, who we are and what we have to offer.

Finding peace or acceptance from within can allow for this transformation to occur. It will only happen when as they say "the time is right." A major life change could be the cause for the awakening to start (death in the family, change in family dynamics, health issues). Once you start to comprehend that something is happening within, allow it to take form. Continue to let the positivity in and drive the negativity out.

EMBRACE THE TRANSFORMATION

Healing comes in time and allowing you that time is so important. We're all different and the healing process is yours and yours only. The loss of a loved one, family transition, job loss or just trying to find your way, is hard.

You must take time to allow your mind, body and soul to heal. The good part is, while doing the healing process, reflection can occur. This gives you a chance to tap into the strength and courage you never knew you had. A different you is already in the making. Embrace the transformation that healing can do.

Death Brings Change

Does death change us? When a loved one leaves this earth does it have a positive or negative effect on you? Of course we would love to have that person for another day but yesterday was that day.

We have a chance now to remember the good times and think about the things learned. That's right, we learn more about ourselves through death. Our perception and perceptive changes, positive or negative is up to you!

Positive Thoughts, Positive Vibes!

For I am convinced
that neither death nor life,
neither angels nor demons,
neither the present nor the future,
nor any powers,
neither height nor depth,
nor anything else in all creation,
will be able to separate us
from the love of God
that is in Christ Jesus our Lord.

START MOVING FORWARD

It's time to do something different. Get out of that rut and start thinking outside of the box. You sit and wish things would change but do nothing about it! Can you see it or maybe feel something new happening? Well, time has come to step out on faith and do it. I get it, still trying to figure out what you will be when you grow up. Well, start doing and you might be surprised. The outcome could be pretty positive. At the end of the day give it your best and make that initial step. Keep moving forward and don't be afraid of the detours, road block or potholes. You're likely to end up on the right path.

POSITIVE THOUGHTS, POSITIVE VIBES!

DON'T

OVER

DO IT

FOCUS ON YOU

You know what? I'm stepping it up today. Going the extra mile, thinking outside the box, being the me I want to be. Don't let the day-to-day tasks of the world bring you down. Slap reality right in the face and put one foot in front of the other. Push a few things aside and get back to being you.

You can only do what you can do! By taking care of yourself you will have the ability to take care of others. Focus on you a little today and allow your positivity to shine through.

POSITIVE THOUGHTS, POSITIVE VIBES!

WHAT IS IMPORTANT TO YOU?

What is really important to You? What are the things that really matter in life? A good job, big house, fancy car? I think what happens is we let "stuff" get in the way. Things seem to be what we feel are important. You keep working towards things that will leave you empty in the end. Maybe today you just need a nice hug, a little breathing room, or an ear to listen. Peace or at least feeling peace might be the most important. Because when we feel peaceful we see the world differently. It gives us the ability to really feel what is important. Simple pleasures are not so hard to come by.

JUST BE YOU

People might ask, "Why do you do the things you do?" Well, I'm just being me. That's right, being you is a cool thing. You know that the ones who want to get it, will get it!

There is no need to compromise your core self to fit in. We all have different qualities about us, so let yours shine. Through that you will attract the right ones and detract the ones not needed in your mix. I'm looking forward to seeing the real you, if you like it, then that's good enough.

POSITIVE THOUGHTS, POSITIVE VIBES!

WORK ON YOU

Are you happy with you? Do you feel good about yourself? I mean, on the inside? How is your spirit, your soul, this is where you need to start. Your spirit and soul must be in the right place for peace.

Peace is a part of happiness
and happiness comes from inner peace.

You must make sure to take time out every day to work on you. Make sure you are giving everything you can through the happiness that comes from the inside.

What an awesome feeling it is to be at peace and happy with who you are.

POSITIVE THOUGHTS, POSITIVE VIBES!

THE GREAT OUTDOORS!

My youngest son, Harrison, loves being outside, whether he's catching bugs or looking for slugs late at night, being outdoors makes him happy.

God's little creatures can offer a sense of gratification. Whether it's riding scooters, or swinging on a swing, take a few minutes to enjoy the peacefulness of the outdoors. It's simplistic, no drama, no over thinking.

Nature allows you to just be and enjoy what life has to offer. You might be surprised how good it makes your spirit feel.

POSITIVE THOUGHTS, POSITIVE VIBES!

SOAK IT ALL IN

Try walking into a crowded room and just taking the time to look around. Soak in your surroundings, listen in on a few conversations, watch people's facial expressions. You can take in and learn more by listening and observing. Sometimes it's best to say less!

You know the saying "What I would give to be a fly on the wall". Heard that one before? Well it's true. Take some time to just listen. Learn through what you hear and what you see. You will be surprised where that experience might take you.

INNER PEACE

Is the ability to have inner peace important to you? If so, what does inner peace feel and look like? Feeling peaceful can sometimes be correlated to being at the beach. The sound of the waves, breeze and the sand in between your feet feel really peaceful.

Inner peace is important because it comes from within. The exterior will look and feel better with inner peace. The true happiness someone feels must come from within first to allow your positive light to shine on the outside.

POSITIVE THOUGHTS, POSITIVE VIBES!

WHAT ARE YOU PRAYING FOR?

You pray and pray but your situation is still the same. You ask God to answer your prayers but nothing is happening. Question? What are you praying for? If your prayer is answered is your soul ready to accept it? Sometimes we need to take a step back and be real about what we're asking God. Maybe order my steps so I can be ready to accept what You have for me.

Your prayer might not be his prayer for you. If you don't open yourself to seeing, you might just miss the little blessing He has all around you. God is ready to help cleanse your soul and have you on the right path made just for you.

TAKE THAT STEP

There's an old saying, "God helps those that help themselves." If you make the first step, He will make the second. So what are you waiting for? They say money doesn't grow on trees, you have to go out and make it.

It's real easy to understand, you must take the lead. Send out that resume, organize the community clean up, start writing that book. Make the first step and then ask God to order your steps in the right direction. You won't know until you try!

STOP WAITING

There's a song that says, "we're waiting on the world to change." Well, I think the change is up to you. You have the power to create the change you want to see in your life.

People will come and go and circumstances might just fuel you forward in making the much needed change. Don't wait for tomorrow when today is right in front of you. Who knows what tomorrow will bring, so if you feel the need now, then do it!

POSITIVE THOUGHTS, POSITIVE VIBES!

The Time is Now!

They say, "take the bull by the horns" and get it done. What are you waiting for? The time is now. You can get it done and get it done, now. Look deep down inside and find the will power to fight through.

Is it fear holding you back? The fear of the unknown? Fear will rob you of the excitement and joy that is waiting for you. Remember that God is always with you, and wants you to get it done. Nike said it best, "Just Do It." Even through failure, the growth will lead you into the positive outcome on the other side. You must try and you must do You!

IT'S TIME!!!

It's time to jump! That's right time to jump. What are you waiting for, the perfect moment, time or place? The stars may never align unless you jump. Yes, you might disappoint a few folks, be judged, or even laughed at. But now is the best time. You will never know what lies ahead if you don't.

Something better is waiting on the other side. Go start that business, write that book, fall in love and even fly across the world. Today is your day to jump into the future with a whole new outlook.

Finally, brothers and sisters,
whatever is true,
whatever is noble,
whatever is right,
whatever is pure,
whatever is lovely,
whatever is admirable
——if anything is excellent
or praiseworthy
——think about such things.

ABOUT THE AUTHOR

His family established the Mitchum Lawn and Landscaping business shortly after. This is where his father, Mitchum Sr. worked for over 30 years, creating beautiful lawns and establishing relationships throughout the community.

Preston Jr. is a graduate of Towson State University where he took his love for video and became an 18 year veteran news photographer for WMAR-TV in Baltimore, Maryland.

During this time, he founded The PMJ Foundation to create change in the Baltimore community. The foundation's vision is to impact families through programs and services that offer positive growth. The foundation has served thousands throughout Maryland.

With the passing of his father, Preston has taken over the family business and will continue to provide the quality service that his family established for many years.

~

A portion of the proceeds of this book
will support the programs that the
PMJ Foundation offers.

~

This book is dedicated to Preston's
two wonderful sons, Carter and Harrison.

~

Preston hopes that the positive message this
book has to offer will impact thousands and
create positive vibes that we all can feel.

THE PMJ FOUNDATION

PRESENTING POSSIBILITIES
FOR BRIGHTER FUTURES

The PMJ Foundation's Career Awareness Project (CAP) after-school program brings the outside professional world into the classroom. Community volunteers present their careers to our participants which engage our at-risk youth to explore the infinite possibilities of college and career choices that are available.

~

To learn more about the PMJ Foundation please visit: **www.pmjfoundation.org**

ERIN GO BRAGH
Publishing

Erin Go Bragh Publishing publishes various genres of books for numerous authors. Their portfolio consists of a 1200 page Vietnamese to English Dictionary, Historical fiction, an award-winning children's educational series, multiple adult novels and memoires, tween adventure stories, as well as Christian Fiction. Their objective is to promote literacy and education through reading and writing.

www.ErinGoBraghPublishing.com
Canyon Lake, Texas

REFERENCES

Made in the USA
Middletown, DE
11 November 2021

52194599R00091